Feng Shui

A Guide For Increased
Real Estate Sales To Asians

Professional
Training Worldwide

Sheida Hodge
14 Aprilla
Irvine, CA 92614
(949) 250-0856
Sheida_Hodge@compuserve.com

Feng Shui
A Guide For Increased
Real Estate Sales To Asians

By Sheida Hodge

Edited By:

Dan Harwig

Published by: **Professional Training Worldwide**
14 Aprilla
Irvine, CA 92614

Hodge, Sheida

Feng Shui: A Guide For Increased Real Estate Sales To Asians
by Sheida Hodge—4th ed.

ISBN 0-9660120-7-0........ $14.95

Includes bibliographic references

1. Feng shui
2. Architecture
3. Interior decoration
4. Real Estate

Table of Contents

Preface

*T*his book is for busy real estate professionals who need to keep up with the latest trends impacting their customers. As the saying goes: "Information is power." This book's aim is to empower you to sell successfully to a rapidly diversifying customer base.

Feng shui (pronounced "fung shway") is the ancient Chinese art of harmonious alignment of the physical environment with positive cosmic forces. It is an essential part of the decision-making process for many Asians buying and selling property, and it is becoming popular with American-born buyers and sellers as well. Donald Trump's well-publicized feng shui consultation and ceremony before renovating the Trump International Tower and Hotel brought this subject into many living rooms.

As Asian and Asian-born investors, buyers and sellers become increasingly active in real estate transactions, real estate professionals need to gain a working knowledge of feng shui.

Although a number of books have been written on feng shui, they are hard to read and the information pertinent to the real estate business is scattered throughout them. I have conducted numerous interviews with Chinese real estate professionals and used their experience with Asian clients to help make sense of what works, what doesn't and what you need to know to make sense of today's real estate market.

The purpose of this book is to give an outline of the rules that most impact the real estate business. It is designed as a working manual to help real estate professionals with Asian clients, but it can also be used to analyze the strengths and weaknesses of properties with an eye to finding feng shui remedies that will help you with all your sales.

For those interested in learning more, a list of additional readings is included at the back of the book.

Introduction

*L*ike it or not, we are faced with concepts, traditions and ideas that just ten years ago were of no concern to us. With record immigration and a shrinking world, we run into each other a lot more. To survive and thrive in this new world we need to understand other people's traditions and ways of thinking.

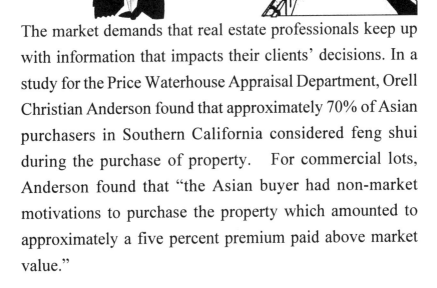

The market demands that real estate professionals keep up with information that impacts their clients' decisions. In a study for the Price Waterhouse Appraisal Department, Orell Christian Anderson found that approximately 70% of Asian purchasers in Southern California considered feng shui during the purchase of property. For commercial lots, Anderson found that "the Asian buyer had non-market motivations to purchase the property which amounted to approximately a five percent premium paid above market value."

A working knowledge of feng shui will help you work with Asian buyers, sellers and investors. And it is increasingly useful for working with American-born clients as well. Your knowledge of feng shui will help build credibility with your clients. You can point out feng shui defects and take steps to remedy them so they do not become a problem during the sales process.

In areas of the country where there are many Asian buyers, non-Asian buyers and owners need to be aware of feng shui defects that may make it difficult to sell their property years later. Listing agents can share this book with their clients to help them understand how feng shui principles affect the sale of their property.

This book will also help you to recognize and point out good feng shui qualities—a strong selling point for many Asian buyers—and make the property attractive to the largest number of potential buyers. Your competence in feng shui will help you get listings and make sales in both the Asian and non-Asian communities.

Our discussion will focus on the following feng shui applications. Remember that the guidelines and rules presented here are not all-inclusive; feng shui principles are subtle and complex, and many depend on specialized knowledge of Chinese astrology.

1. Basic principles of feng shui

2. Building site and location

3. Building configuration

4. Building interiors

5. Commercial real estate

Also included in this new edition is a chapter outlining the basic principles of doing business with customers with Asian cultural roots. Included are strategies for establishing trust and credibility, tips about how to handle particular cultural differences, how Asian clients come to a decision about a purchase, and tips for dealing with language and accent barriers.

Basic Principles of Feng Shui

The art of living in harmony with the land, and deriving the greatest benefit, peace and prosperity from being in the right place at the right time is called feng shui.
—Stephen Skinner

Feng Shui Schools

Feng shui can be traced back at least 2,000 years. Its development and practice reflect centuries of common sense, tradition, superstition and astrology.

In addition to the Chinese, feng shui has adherents among other Asians, such as Koreans, Vietnamese and Japanese. In the United States, feng shui is used in the selection, location and design of homes, restaurants, stores and office buildings from Boston to Vancouver to Los Angeles.

Feng shui has evolved through the years. There are traditional adherents of feng shui as well as reform-minded practitioners. Feng shui professionals can be called in for consultation on more technical aspects and problems, but there is also wide-spread knowledge passed down through family and folk traditions. Beliefs can vary from one region or country to the next, but they share a common set of basic principles.

There is also a growing Americanized version of feng shui practiced by and for Americans. In the coming years, you may be bombarded with a lot of information about feng shui that might confuse and mislead you.

One of the best ways to learn about feng shui is to listen to your Asian customers and pay attention to their preferences. Families and individuals are sensitive to different areas of feng shui. Traditions are passed down orally from one generation to the next, and there can be a good deal of variation in individual beliefs. Feng shui defects that might be very offensive to one customer might not bother another. You need to create a climate in which your clients feel comfortable telling you their preferences.

Remember that as a real estate professional your clients don't expect you to be a professional feng shui advisor. You wouldn't give legal advice to your clients unless you were a lawyer; nor should you give definitive feng shui advice.

Traditional feng shui uses a luopan (a kind of compass) to determine the best direction, location and orientation of a home or office. This method relies heavily on calculating the relationships of yin and yang, the five elements, the eight trigrams, the geographical orientation and the influence of the heavens.

More Americanized systems have stopped using the compass altogether, saying that in the modern world electricity interferes with the earth's magnetic flow—rendering the compass ineffective. American feng shui tends to be more liberal and intuitive—often using mirrors, crystals, wind chimes, plants and fountains to remedy feng shui defects.

Caveat: Not all Asians believe in feng shui, and some may be insulted if you assume they do. Some who profess not to believe may have silent preferences. Some who don't believe may have relatives involved in the purchasing decision who do. In general, it's best to wait until clients bring up the subject—though you can find subtle ways to let them know you are familiar with the tradition.

Yin and Yang

*F*eng shui means "wind and water." It is utilized to enhance the beneficial aspects of nature and the cosmos while protecting against harmful elements. Its main purpose is alignment with the environment and living in harmony and balance with nature.

The primary application of feng shui is proper, harmonious placement—the proper siting of a building, its architectural configuration and its interior layout.

The concept of feng shui is based on ancient Chinese Taoist philosophy. Taoism divides the universe into two primal forces—yin and yang. Yin is dark, female and passive. Yang is light, male and active. For the Chinese, the ideal environment is one that balances the forces of yin and yang.

Good feng shui means balancing yin and yang in one's environment. A dark and gloomy house or building has excessive yin energy and will lead to depression. An overly bright, geometric environment—as in some modernist designs—has too much yang energy, which leads to agitation and a sense of unease.

Yin and yang complement each other to form a complete and balanced environment. One cannot exist without the other, and each contains an element of the other. When yin and yang are in balance, there is good ch'i or "breath of life."

Yin and yang each have their proper place in our lives. The "coziness" of a yin environment is a good place to retreat from the world. Yang environments are good places to work or meet people. Many people have either yin or yang preferences; some gravitate to yin environments that others find gloomy and oppressive. Others are at home in yang environments that drive yin people crazy. Finding the right balance of yin and yang for any person or environment requires a good deal of sensitivity and intuition.

The following list outlines some of the attributes and environments associated with yin and yang:

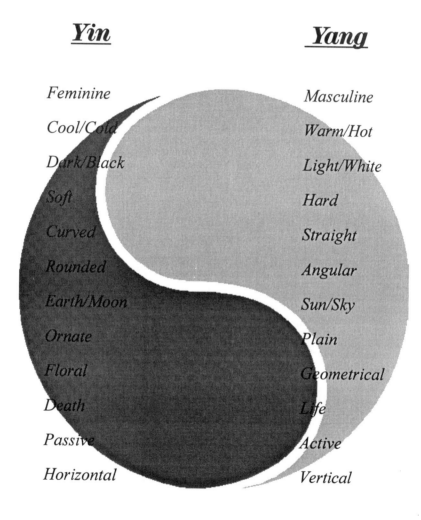

___Yin___	___Yang___
Feminine	Masculine
Cool/Cold	Warm/Hot
Dark/Black	Light/White
Soft	Hard
Curved	Straight
Rounded	Angular
Earth/Moon	Sun/Sky
Ornate	Plain
Floral	Geometrical
Death	Life
Passive	Active
Horizontal	Vertical

The Five Elements

*Y*in and yang express themselves in the universe through five elements: wood, fire, earth, metal and water. The interactions of these elements determine the harmony between yin and yang. An environment with good feng shui blends the five elements to produce a naturally balanced whole. The five elements are related to each other in a cycle in which each element generates the next:

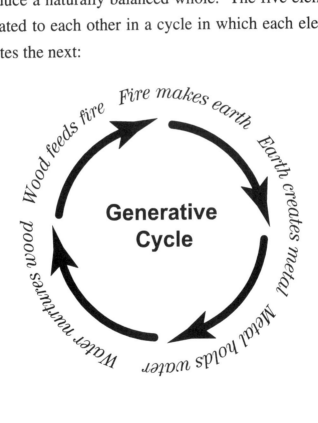

The elements are also related by a controlling cycle:

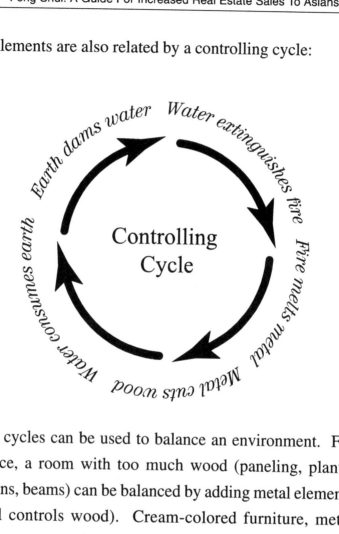

These cycles can be used to balance an environment. For instance, a room with too much wood (paneling, plants, columns, beams) can be balanced by adding metal elements (metal controls wood). Cream-colored furniture, metal sculpture or natural crystals help control the wood element. Water elements (which nurture wood) should also be controlled to prevent the room from turning into a "jungle."

The five elements are associated with *directions, seasons* and *colors*:

Element	Wood	Fire	Earth	Metal	Water
Direction	East	South	Center	West	North
Season	Spring	Summer		Autumn	Winter
Color	Green	Red	Yellow	White	Black

Note for real estate professionals: Earth is the element representing those engaged in buying, selling, developing, designing or contracting buildings or real estate. It is considered auspicious for these people to activate the "earth" sectors of their office: the center and the south-western and north-eastern corners. It is considered wise to locate crucial business activities in these areas. Earth elements such as natural quartz crystals or stone carvings enhance this effect.

Attributes of the Five Elements

Wood

Wooden furniture
Wooden panelling
Indoor plants
Cotton cloth
Floral prints
Landscape art
Columns, beams
Blue, green

Fire

Lighting, sunlight
Fireplaces, candles
Fur, leather, bone
Pets and wildlife
People, animal art
Fire, sun in art
Triangles, pyramids
Reds

Earth

Adobe, brick, tile
Ceramics, pottery
Squares, rectangles
Landscape art
Yellow, earth tones
Deserts in art

Metal

Steel, copper, brass
Rocks, stone, marble
Granite, flagstone
Art of stone or metal
Whites, pastels
Circles, ovals, arches

Water

Streams, rivers
Cut crystal
Flowing free forms
Circles, ovals, arches

Fountains, pools
Glass, mirrors
Black , dark-tone colors
Charcoal gray

(Based on A Western Guide to Feng Shui *by Terah Kathryn Collins)*

Feng Shui and Ch'i

Ch'i is the central concept of feng shui. Ch'i can be translated as "breath," "wind" or "life force." Ch'i brings health, prosperity and happiness. Ch'i is ephemeral. It is cosmic and, at the same time, of this world. It is energy, spirit and matter. It flows everywhere, across the land, the heavens, the rivers, and through the human body. It swirls around us and through us.

Good ch'i flows smoothly, not too swiftly, not too slowly. If its current is too fast, it becomes bad ch'i or "sha ch'i." If it flows too slowly, there is inadequate life force. When trees and flowers bloom and people thrive, it's a sign of good ch'i.

Feng shui is used to regulate the flow of ch'i in one's environment. Building design and configuration, the placement of objects and the relations between yin and yang and the five elements affect the way ch'i "flows" through a house. A dresser that prevents a door from opening fully or a table in the middle of a natural walkway interrupt the smooth flow of ch'i through the house.

Light, air and beautiful scenery are sources of good ch'i— energy that invigorates and purifies one's environment. On the other hand, a busy street can produce an overpowering, negative flow of ch'i that can be damaging if it is not deflected or controlled.

Feng Shui and Architectural Design

*F*eng shui can also be understood as a collection of common-sense design principles. The "flow of ch'i" and "balancing the five elements" are simply a different language for talking about how the various parts of our environment are related to each other and the psychological effects they have on us.

Feng shui stresses the intuitive feelings picked up from different places or designs. A place that brings about a sense of foreboding is to be avoided. Places and situations that give a sense of happiness and comfort are desirable. Feng shui masters have developed their senses to be particularly sensitive to the environment, enabling them to pick up messages and signs from their surroundings.

More and more builders are incorporating feng shui principles into the design of their homes. (It would be hard to find a new home in Southern California in which the stairs faced the front door.)

Good feng shui can enhance the sale and resale value of a property because the design principles it embodies have widespread appeal for Westerners as well as Asians. Many people—especially Asians—will pay top dollar for a property with good feng shui.

Building Site and Location

A s all real estate professionals know, location is everything. A good feng shui site is in harmony with nature and neighboring properties. It facilitates the beneficial flow of ch'i and does not incur bad omens.

• In traditional feng shui, the most appropriate location and orientation for a structure is determined according to the owner's date and time of birth. (See the charts on page 80.) Apartments and houses facing south are generally preferred. In some Chinese cities, apartments facing south command higher rental prices.

• High ground and undulating land are preferred over valleys or low-lying land.

• Good influences accumulate when a building is backed on the north by a mountain with smaller hills on both sides.

- The back yard should be slightly but not too much larger than the front yard. This helps the accumulation of wealth.

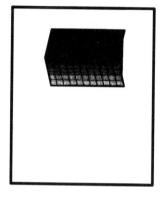

House built too far back on lot.

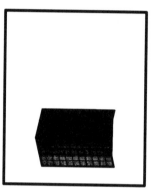

House built too far forward on lot.

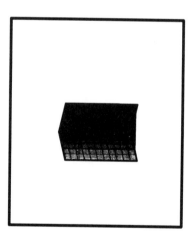

House centered on lot. Back yard is slightly larger than front yard to offer protection and help the accumulation of wealth.

- Healthy trees, particularly on the north-west side of the site, indicate good ch'i. They symbolize protection.

- Hills on the northern side of the house with vacant land sloping toward water represent an ideal site. Hills on the north side protect homes from bad influences. When good ch'i flows downhill to the south, the family will be healthy.

- Water should be clean and free-flowing. Dirty, stagnant water can create sha ch'i (poisonous breath).

- Houses embraced by a road or body of water help gather ch'i. This promotes health and the accumulation of wealth.

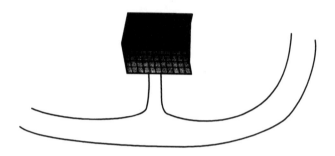

- Houses with one-way streets flowing away from the entrance will draw ch'i out of the house, leading to loss of wealth.

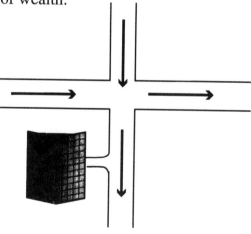

- Houses facing the "blade" of a road bring sickness and poverty.

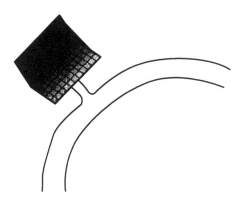

- Secret arrows—such as sharp edges of roofs, chimneys or sides of nearby buildings which point directly at the site—are undesirable. (Such structures are thought to symbolize enemy bowmen poised to unleash arrows.) To ward off this harmful ch'i, a bagua (an octagonal mirror) can be mounted at the top of the front door or some other strategic spot.

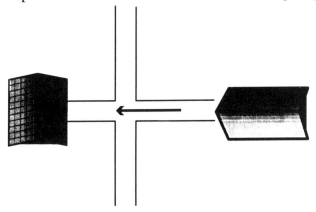

• A home or apartment building with a street pointed directly at it—such as a cul-de-sac or T intersection—is unlucky. It is also bad to have the driveway pointed directly at the front door.

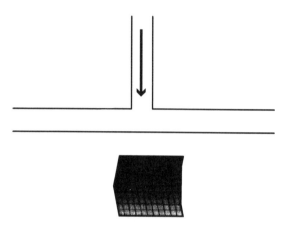

• Dagger-like roads facing a house lead to ill fortune or death.

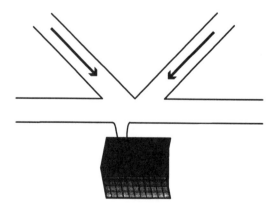

- A building at the intersection of a "Y" junction will bring the occupants bad luck.

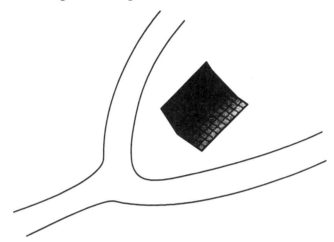

- Square or rectangular lots are generally best. Lots with triangular or irregular shapes should be avoided. However, feng shui construction and landscaping can help enhance overall proportion and balance in awkward sites.

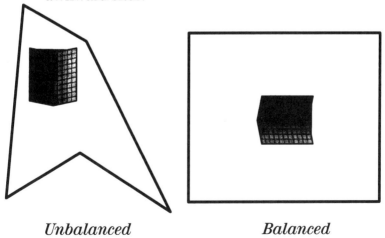

Unbalanced   *Balanced*

- Curved driveways optimize the flow of ch'i.

- An ideal landscape is a hilly terrain that exhibits dragon-, tiger-, turtle- and/or phoenix-shaped contours. Hills on the northern side with vacant land sloping to the south toward water represent an ideal site. Hills on the north side protect homes from bad influences. When good ch'i flows downhill to the south, the family will be happy.

Good Feng Shui Omens

*T*he health and prosperity of former owners or occupants can affect the feng shui of a location or neighborhood. A death in the house is considered unlucky. It is good to purchase a home when the owners are moving because of an enlarged family or business success.

- Neighboring homes can influence the feng shui of a house. Neighborhoods have a flow of ch'i that connects and affects individual homes. Harmonious placement of houses with respect to each other and the streets helps determine the feng shui of a location.

- A winding path leading to a well-proportioned entrance is ideal.

- Hills or a mountain behind the house—especially on the north side—are a good omen.

- Thriving trees and plants, especially natural vegetation, are a sign of good ch'i. The wise use of plants and landscaping can improve the feng shui of a location by creating natural, harmonious divisions of the space, by ensuring privacy, and by covering inauspicious elements in the landscape.

- Animals bring good ch'i, especially beautiful birds or deer. Fish and fish ponds also have good feng shui.

Bad Feng Shui Omens

*M*omentary feelings of foreboding or anxiety can be a sign of bad feng shui. Pay attention to the "feeling" you get from a property. Your unconscious mind is often aware of problems that don't show on the surface.

- The front portion of the lot should not be higher than the rear. (Negative ch'i can collect or "pool" in the back of the property.)

- Proximity to or view of a cemetery is a bad omen.

- A large pole or tree blocking the front door is poor feng shui.

- Investigating a property on a stormy or overcast day is inauspicious. The morning of a calm, sunny day (before the light gets too bright to judge the yin-yang balance) is ideal.

- Property next to jagged hills or rough, broken mountains is bad luck.

- Proximity to garbage dumps or slums, naturally enough, is a bad omen.

- A swimming pool on the top of a hill or apartment building is inauspicious. The water above is considered dangerous.

- A house at the top of an exposed mountain is hazardous. Ch'i is rapidly dispersed and drained away.

- Buildings or properties overshadowed by a cross are inauspicious. The situation is especially bad if the shadow of the cross falls on the house.

- Avoid locations that are too exposed to the elements such as cliffs, locations close to the sea, or buildings near the flood plains of rivers.

- Avoid locating a house near a road that has been cut into the side of a hill or mountain, particularly if red earth has been exposed. (This indicates an injury to the dragon of the mountain.)

- A house under the outside edge of a freeway flyover is extremely dangerous.

- Mirrors generally have very good feng shui. But they can be dangerous in bedrooms, especially if they are placed in such a way that you can see yourself from the bed.

Building Configuration

The overall shape and configuration of a building is an important feng shui consideration. A good configuration should balance the five elements, promote the circulation of ch'i and create harmony with the surrounding environment. The same general rules apply to apartment shapes.

Irregular shapes with many sharp angles are undesirable. Square or circular designs are best.

The layout of rooms can be analyzed using the bagua map on page 73. A schematic plan of the building should be placed entirely within the bagua rectangle. If the building is irregularly shaped, and parts of the map fall outside the building outline, the space is still part of the basic bagua plan.

The "love & marriage" section of my friend's home, for instance, is occupied by a heavy-duty exterior air conditioning unit that lies in an angular indentation cutting into the right-rear corner of her home. She blames this arrangement for a chilling effect on her romantic endeavors. (She has recently taken steps to "warm up" this important part of her bagua space.)

In general, it is desirable to devote parts of the house to activities that correspond to the bagua map. Of course, it is almost never possible to have things match up exactly, but you can often take steps to improve the correspondence (locating bookshelves in the "knowledge & self-cultivation" section or placing flowers or plants in the "health & family" area).

Building Shape

structure that is much taller or shorter than surrounding buildings is not desirable. Building size and architectural style should be in harmony with other buildings in the area. When the Bank of China built a blade-like skyscraper jutting out of the center of Hong Kong, nearby residents and businesses complained that it destroyed the feng shui of their 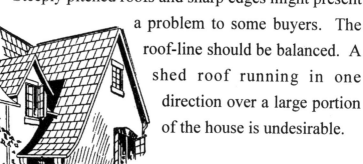 buildings. The skyscraper has had poor occupancy and a reputation for bad luck for tenants.

- Steeply pitched roofs and sharp edges might present a problem to some buyers. The roof-line should be balanced. A shed roof running in one direction over a large portion of the house is undesirable.

- Symmetrical buildings—square, rectangular, or circular—are ideal. L-shaped, U-shaped or other irregular buildings are less desirable.

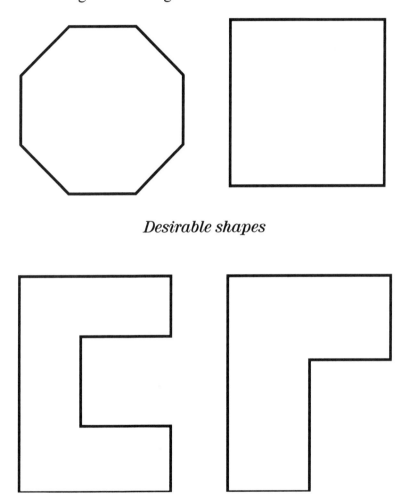

Desirable shapes

Undesirable shapes

- An irregular building can be improved by adding a patio, deck, veranda or landscaping that balances the building and ties the space together.

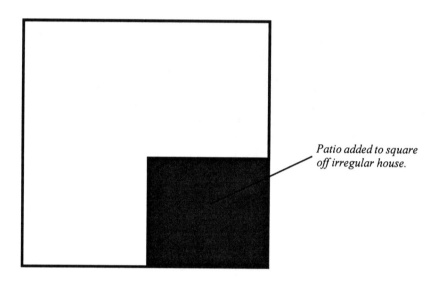

Patio added to square off irregular house.

Doors and Entrances

$\mathcal{F}$he front door should face the direction determined to be auspicious by the feng shui master. For general purposes, south is the best direction. See the charts on page 80 to find the orientation that corresponds to your date and time of birth.

• A double-door entrance is more favorable because it is symmetrical; however, all entrance doors should be pleasingly proportional to the building dimensions.

• Doors should be wide enough to let ch'i enter easily. They should not be obstructed by large trees, columns or poles.

Balanced entrance

Narrow, unbalanced entrance

- A porch or veranda with space to place a few chairs or flowers helps tie the interior of the house to its exterior environment.

- If the entry has a peaked roof or canopy, there will be lawsuits.

- Solid doors are preferable to see-through, especially for interior doors. Wood is preferable to glass or steel.

- The front door should not be in line with rear doors or windows because ch'i will rush straight through and not circulate. Remedies include interior screens and hanging chimes.

Window

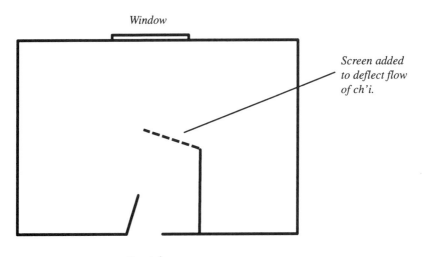

Screen added to deflect flow of ch'i.

Front door

• When the front door is too large you may place a wind chime in the front hall to defuse strong ch'i currents.

• If the entrance to an apartment lies at the end of a long corridor, the ch'i can become too fierce. This torrent can be slowed by placing a plant or wind chimes in the hallway.

• The path to the entrance should not be a straight line. Curved, meandering paths are favored.

Windows

C h'i flows into and out of buildings through doors and windows. Small windows or doors can choke off the flow of ch'i into a building. On the other hand, overly large windows—despite their "spectacular" views—can pull too much ch'i out of the room, or flood it with excess yang energy. The movement of ch'i from doors to windows should follow a clear but meandering path.

- Windows that open completely are preferable to those that slide up and down. Inward-opening windows are considered harmful to careers, and opportunities to make money will be damaged. Outward-opening windows are the most auspicious.

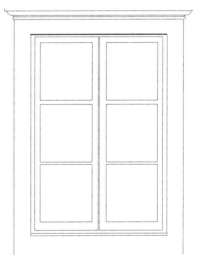

- Windows that face west are not generally favored— especially in hot climates, where they allow in too much afternoon sun. This defect can be remedied by hanging heavy curtains during summer months, or by planting trees or shrubbery to shield the windows from the sun.

- Windows opening onto busy streets allow in excessive amounts of bad ch'i created by the heavy traffic.

- The size of windows should be proportional to the size of the room on the inside and to the face of the building on the outside. Large windows can be divided into sections or panes. Too few windows or windows that are too small can restrict the flow of ch'i.

*Small windows and wall blocking the front door
create a fort-like feel to this house.*

Garages

arages have become an increasingly important feature of modern houses. Many have large two- or three-car garages jutting out toward the street, while the front door is recessed or even hidden altogether. This may be convenient, but having a huge threatening "mouth" dominating the front of the house cuts off the organic connection between the inside of the house and its environment.

Garage-dominated house

- If you are building your own house, the side or back of the property is the best place to locate the garage. If you do put it in the front, be sure it does not jut out, dominate the front of the house or overpower the front porch and door.

- Paint the garage the same color as the house to help tie the two together.

- If the front door is recessed, you can help "bring it forward" by adding a deck, patio or porch. Plants and fences can be used to draw attention and ch'i from the garage and direct it toward the real entrance to the house.

- The garage should be cleaned up and organized. Like basements, garages tend to accumulate clutter and negative ch'i. Periodic clean-ups are a healthy feng shui exercise.

- If there is an interior door from the garage into the house, it should be given the symbolic status of an entry door. You don't want to feel like you're sneaking out through a closet every time you leave the house. Installing a carved panel door, painting the trim a different color, placing a light over the door or otherwise calling attention to it are possible solutions.

Fences and Walls

*F*ences and walls can serve as effective barriers against harmful influences. However, they need to be harmoniously integrated into the landscape and placed in such a way that they do not hem the house in or cut off beneficial flows of ch'i. Trees or other foliage can help balance brick walls or fences.

- Metal fences should not have spikes pointing downwards (which signifies dissent) or inwards (which forms "poison arrows" directed at the occupants). Spikes pointed upwards are considered neutral.

- Hedges or other foliage can often substitute for fences or walls.

Building Interiors

*B*uilding interiors should be compatible with the occupants' horoscopes, the flow of ch'i and other rules of good fortune. Yin and yang and the five elements should be balanced. Rooms can be balanced both internally and with each other. For instance, a very yang living room might be balanced with a cozy yin TV room or den.

- Entranceways should be light, open and inviting. The main door should open inwards and give a view of as much of the house as possible. Avoid lobbies with low ceilings or narrow walls. A mirror can be used to expand a confined entrance way.

- Interiors should be light but subdued. Harsh shadows, colors and textures should be avoided.

- Dark rooms inhibit the flow of ch'i. Unobtrusive light fixtures or mirrors can be used to enhance a dark room. Low-hanging light fixtures are harmful. Rooms that are open and airy are ideal—though too many windows can let out ch'i too quickly.

- Mirrors can be used to deflect harmful forces or to create a sense of space and draw positive forces into a home or office.

- Water, whether viewed through a window or reflected by a mirror, is believed to cause money to flow in. Clean, healthy fish tanks are sometimes used as a substitute for an exterior source.

- Staircases should not face the front entrance or start immediately outside the master bedroom. Stairs that fit into the natural design of the house rather than intruding into the living space are best.

Staircase does not intrude into living area or face the front door. The landing midway creates a meandering flow of ch'i.

- Curved or angled staircases rather than straight staircases are best—but not if they intrude into the living space. Spiral staircases (which symbolically resemble corkscrews) are dangerous, especially in the center of the house.

Corkscrew staircase intruding into living area.

- Heavy beams exert too much ch'i pressure on a room and its occupants. Beams are especially harmful when situated over an entrance, a bed, a stove, or above the dining room table. Hanging flutes, draperies or plants can sometimes alleviate the problem. A traditional remedy is to place pieces of bamboo at an angle to the beam itself—thus breaking the flow of ch'i along the beam. Painting beams a light color that blends with the surroundings can help soften their presence.

- Slanted walls, doors and beams are bad for feng shui. Rooms with slanted or non-parallel walls should be "squared off" or otherwise symmetrically proportioned with curtains, screens, plants or hanging tassels.

- Two or three doors in a row are bad feng shui. Place a screen, a large plant or a fish tank between doors to correct this problem.

- Long, narrow rooms or overly tall rooms (such as those found in some modern designs) can throw off the feng shui of a home. Overly tall ceilings can be lowered with hanging plants—or by an indoor tree to tie the space together.

- Door size should be proportional to the size of the room. Large doors should always lead to large rooms.

- The dining room should be next to or near the kitchen. Bedrooms and bathrooms should be farther away.

- Fireplaces, bathrooms, bedrooms and staircases should not face the front door.

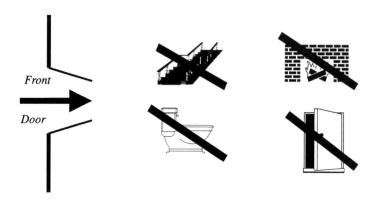

- Much modern architecture is dominated by angular, geometric shapes. Sharp corners that jut into rooms threaten the occupants and undercut ch'i. Sharp angles can be rounded with furniture or softened with plants.

- Doors, windows, walls, roofs and plumbing should be maintained in excellent condition. "Fixer-upper" homes are not generally favored by Asians.

- Some Asian customers may prefer new homes because they present a clean slate. The buyer won't be affected by the troubles of previous occupants.

●   Plants create ch'i and help distribute it. They are particularly effective when placed in corners or used to camouflage sharp room edges.

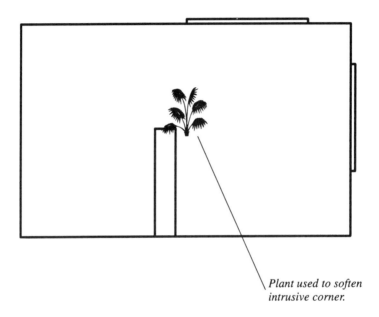

Plant used to soften intrusive corner.

Bedrooms

*T*o prevent arguments between family members, it is best to have all bedrooms on one side of the hall. Bedroom doors should not face each other directly. If they do, a wind chime or mobile can be used to break up the direct line of contact.

- Mirrors should not face the bed, particularly the foot of a bed. In bedrooms with several sliding mirrored doors over a closet or wardrobe, it may be necessary to replace them with wood or painted doors.

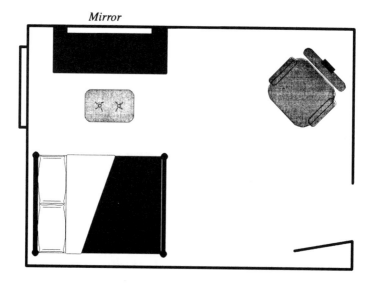

Dangerous bedroom configuration

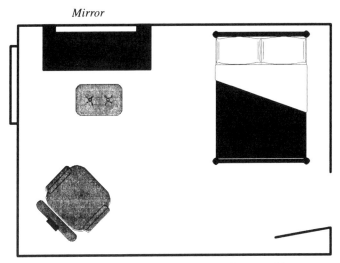

Mirror

Auspicious bedroom configuration

- Beds should be oriented so the feet don't point toward the door. (Traditionally, the dead are laid out in this fashion.)

- In Japan, sleeping with your head to the north and your feet to the south is considered bad luck.

- It is best not to have childrens' bedrooms over a garage.

- Sleeping under beams or steeply sloped roofs is considered unlucky.

Bathrooms

*T*raditional Chinese homes rarely had indoor bathrooms. Placing them inside has created numerous problems for modern houses. One cure recommended by modern feng shui practitioners is hiding the toilet from view with a divider or by recessing it.

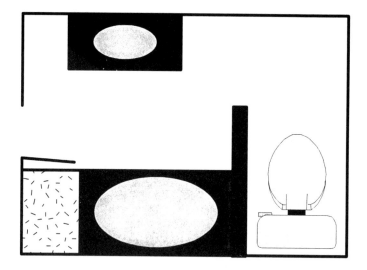

- A bathroom should not face the front door. If this occurs, a mirror on the exterior of the bathroom door can improve the situation.

- Bathroom drains can siphon ch'i out of the house. It is best to keep drains—especially the toilet—covered when not in use.

- A bathroom off the master bedroom should have a door to avoid having one's wealth flushed down the drain.

- Problems can result from bathrooms located in the marriage or family corners of the house. (In fact, bathrooms are a problem wherever they are located. It is often necessary to simply choose the least damaging location.)

Kitchens

*T*he kitchen is a symbol of the family's health, wealth and prosperity. It should be well lit and regular in shape.

- The cooking area should not be too close to the sink. The clash of fire and water elements leads to bad feng shui.

- Work areas should be placed so that the cook does not have his or her back to the entry door.

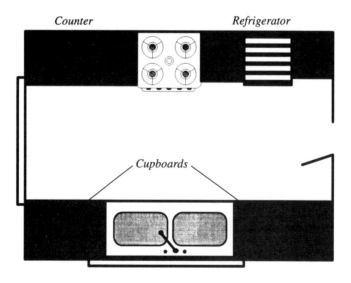

A good kitchen layout

- The best location for the kitchen is in the south end of the house, with the exception of the south-west corner (a configuration that combines too many fire elements).

- "Poison arrows" are especially common in kitchens. Sharp angles from cupboards or appliances can cause unhappiness or ill health. Rounded cabinets, plants or other feng shui remedies can help alleviate problems.

- Open cabinet shelves can produce sha ch'i (poison breath) directed at those working in the kitchen. Covered cabinets are preferable.

Placement of Furniture

If you want change in your life, move twenty-seven things in your house.
—Chinese proverb

*P*lacement of furniture is an important part of feng shui. Moving around furniture, wall hangings, plants, sculpture and fish tanks can often dramatically change the look and feel of a room. Ch'i should be able to flow freely through a room. Furniture that blocks natural walkways, overly cluttered spaces, or furniture that prevents doors from opening fully are especially harmful.

- The ideal shape for a dining table is round (symbolizing heaven). Dining chairs should come in pairs of four, six or eight. (Luck comes in pairs; single numbers represent loneliness.)

- Avoid placing chairs or sofas under heavy beams.

•   Furniture should be arranged so that sharp angles don't point at doors—especially bedroom doors.

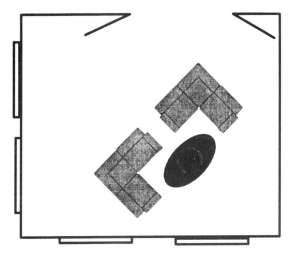

Harmful configuration

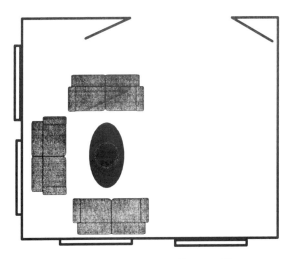

Auspicious configuration

Commercial Real Estate

*C*ommercial buildings are evaluated using the same general criteria as homes. The design and placement of a building should be harmonious with the type of business it contains. The composition of the five elements in the building should be chosen to nurture the product or service offered by the business.

A pharmacy, for instance, is concerned with healing and growth—a wood function. In the generative cycle (see page 17), water nurtures wood. Therefore, water elements would be helpful to enhance this particular business.

An employment agency is based on communication. Communication is a water element. In the generative cycle, metal holds water, calling for an accentuation of metal elements in the design of a building.

The chart on the next page shows the relationship between the elements and some common businesses. When the situation is complex—when there are several businesses located in one building or a business has several different functions—it is best to consult a feng shui master for detailed advice.

Business	Element	Business	Element
Advertising	Water	Jewellery	Metal
Artist studio	Wood	Laundry	Water
Cafe	Wood	Intellectual occupations	Fire
Carpentry	Wood	Literature and publishing	Water
Construction	Earth	Media-related businesses	Water
Civil engineering	Earth	Financial services	Metal
Communications	Water	Music	Water
Computers	Water	Nurseries, gardening	Wood
Distilling	Water	Oil wells	Water
Electricity	Water	Railroads	Metal
Farming	Earth	Restaurants	Wood
Forges	Fire	Storage	Earth
Hardware	Metal	Word processing	Water
Hospitals	Wood	Workshops	Metal

• A business should be located at an intersection or confluence of streets that gathers ch'i and people into a central location. This helps channel people into the building and aids the accumulation of wealth.

From Feng Shui: The Chinese Art of Placement *by Sara Rossbach.*

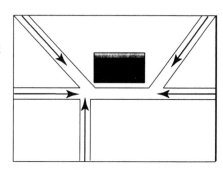

• Wide entrances under a gently sloping roof draw in ch'i, money and people.

The RE/MAX office in Irvine, CA is a very good feng shui building. The wide entrances and corner location work to draw ch'i into the building.

- A building should be in harmony with its environment and surrounding buildings. When the Bank of China built an office tower in Hong Kong, many neighbors complained that it destroyed the feng shui of the neighborhood. According to American feng shui practitioner Derek Walters, the Bank of China's building deliberately incorporated triangular elements associated with metal into its design. The smaller buildings surrounding it were like a forest of trees. Since wood feeds fire, and fire creates metal, the Bank of China's design worked to enrich it at the expense of its neighbors.

- A withered or awkwardly shaped tree in front of the building interrupts the flow of ch'i (and wealth) into the building. However, buildings framed by healthy trees are embraced and protected.

- Straight lines directed at the entrance—such as those produced by roads, walkways or the corner of another building—can produce sha ch'i. Entrances should not be obstructed by a flagpole or a wall. Doors can be set at an angle to help alleviate these problems. If this is not practical, mirrors or other feng shui remedies can be used.

- Buildings can be either yin or yang depending on their function. Businesses that are closed and protective such as banks and jewellery stores do best in protected, yin buildings. Merchants that sell consumer goods such as food, clothes or hardware directly to the public are better in yang buildings that draw the customer in. The bookstore in the photo below "exteriorizes" itself in yang fashion to draw people in from the street.

- Initial impressions are important for success in business. Chinese commercial buildings often place indoor gardens, fish tanks or ponds near the entrance to produce a good flow of ch'i and a positive impression on the customer. These ornamental elements can also be used to enhance the elements that are most beneficial for a specific business.

- Groups of buildings should be balanced and harmonious. The most important buildings should be at the center. It is a good idea to have unifying architectural features to tie the buildings together.

- Glass buildings produce glare—sha ch'i—that can harm neighboring buildings and hurt the feng shui of the area.

- T-junctions at the front of buildings can cause ch'i to be drawn out of the building. Buildings oriented slightly at an angle can help offset this effect. If this is not possible, putting the entrances at an angle can help.

- Triangular lots are especially bad for commercial buildings. They interrupt the harmonious flow of ch'i—and the space is hard to use effectively.

- Creating green areas such as gardens or plazas can help improve the feng shui of high-rises and large corporate buildings. Such green areas retain ch'i better if they are clearly defined by borders or boundaries.

Additional Feng Shui Information

*Y*ou can use the bagua map on the following page to determine the bagua areas for your entire house or to map individual rooms or sections. The bagua configuration of the entire building is more important than the bagua values of any particular room. Feng shui masters use the bagua map to locate problems and suggest possible solutions.

If the occupants are having trouble in family life, for instance, it may be because the section of the house representing to Health & Family is cluttered or choked off. Perhaps there is a bathroom there and the family's ch'i is being dragged "down the drain." Appropriate remedies might include adding windows or doors, putting plants, fish tanks or mirrors, or simply cleaning up and organizing the area.

The Bagua Rectangle

Wealth & Prosperity	Fame & Reputation	Love & Marriage
Health & Family	Center	Creativity & Children
Knowledge & Self-Cultivation	Career	Helpful People & Travel

Entrance

(*Based on* A Western Guide to Feng Shui *by Terah Kathryn Collins*)

Feng Shui Remedies

*T*he following items can be used to alleviate or disguise feng shui defects by balancing the yin and yang of a room or building, harmonizing the five elements, attracting positive ch'i or warding off harmful influences such as "poison arrows" and negative flows of ch'i.

Mirrors	*Aquariums*
Crystals	*Mobiles*
Wind chimes	*Fountains*
Bagua octagons	*Bamboo flutes*
Trees	*Statues*
Plants	*Stones*
Screens	*Flowers*

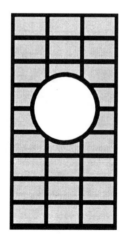

Numbers, Colors and Patterns

ccording to Taoist philosophy, odd numbers are yang (male) and even numbers are yin (female).   Numbers have different connotations in the various Asian countries.

- One in the Chinese tradition signifies heaven, beginnings and birth.

- Four signifies death to the Chinese, Japanese, Vietnamese and Koreans. Don't give gifts in groups of four. House numbers that contain fours or groups of fours may be rejected by many Asians. A group of numbers that adds up to four might be considered unlucky.

- Five is a lucky number according to the Chinese and the Japanese. It is associated with the five elements of nature. However, in some dialects the word for "five" sounds like "not." Some Chinese might not like it if a five is placed next to a lucky number. For instance, eight is a lucky number signifying prosperity. But 58—5 + 8—could equate to "not prospering."

- Eight is a very lucky number. Consider using eights for listing the sales price of the home if there are many Asian buyers. You might also consider using eights for counteroffers to Asian sellers.

- Nine is a very popular number with the Chinese, who associate it with longevity and dragons. However, for the Japanese, nines signify misery and suffering.

- Ten in Chinese sounds like "sure" or "guaranteed." When a "10" is combined with another number, it suggests a guarantee of that number's meaning. Fourteen—10 + 4—means "guaranteed death."

*C*olors have associations with yin and yang and the five elements. Colors and combinations of colors are an important part of balancing an environment. Rooms should not be too hot (red or yellow) or too cold (blue, green or white). A pleasant balance of yin and yang colors and light is most desirable. Dramatic colors can be used if they are balanced with other colors or elements and integrated harmoniously into the environment.

- Red is auspicious and connotes happiness, warmth and all good things in life. Deep reds and purples inspire great respect. However, some Chinese might not like to write with a red pen or sign their name in red ink.

- Gold and yellow represent wealth, authority and longevity. Red and gold make a good combination.

- Green connotes tranquility, potency and longevity resulting from healthy earth ch'i.

- Blue is a secondary Chinese mourning color and is not recommended for use with white. Blue is often used with other colors, however. The Japanese especially favor blue.

- Black and red are lucky in combination. By itself, black signifies death and dark times and should be avoided.

- White is associated with purity. It is an important color at funerals. Unbleached white muslin is worn by Chinese mourners and the funeral is decorated in yellow and white. White or white and yellow combinations of flowers should not be given as gifts. Also, gifts should not be wrapped in white, or white and yellow wrapping paper. A very white room can be enhanced and balanced with warm yang colors.

*P*atterns on walls, floors, furniture and ceilings also have symbolism. The table below illustrates various decorative patterns which bring good fortune.

Pattern	Significance
Elephant	*Wisdom*
Pine tree	*Longevity & endurance*
Vase	*Peace*
Phoenix & dragon	*Balance of yin and yang*
Fish scale	*Success*
Lotus	*Endurance and uprightness*
Water ripples	*Wealth and heavenly bliss*
Clouds	*Heavenly blessing, wisdom*
Flowers	*Wealth*
Tortoise shell	*Longevity*
Old coins	*Wealth*
Bats	*Luck*
Cranes	*Fidelity, honesty, longevity*
Deer	*Wealth*

Entrance Orientations

The following charts give the ideal entrance orientations for houses based on the owner's year of birth.

Ideal Orientations for Women

	SE	E	SW	N	S	NE	W	NW	NW
Year of Birth	1917	1916	1915	1914	1913	1912	1911	1910	1909
	1926	1925	1924	1923	1922	1921	1920	1919	1918
	1935	1934	1933	1932	1931	1930	1929	1928	1927
	1944	1943	1942	1941	1940	1939	1938	1937	1936
	1953	1952	1951	1950	1949	1948	1947	1946	1945
	1962	1961	1960	1959	1958	1957	1956	1955	1954
	1971	1970	1969	1968	1967	1966	1965	1964	1963
	1980	1979	1978	1977	1976	1975	1974	1973	1972
	1989	1988	1987	1986	1985	1984	1983	1982	1981
	1998	1997	1996	1995	1994	1993	1992	1991	1990
	2007	2006	2005	2004	2003	2002	2001	2000	1999
	2016	2015	2014	2013	2012	2011	2010	2009	2008

Ideal Orientations for Men

	SW	E	SE	SW	NW	W	NE	S	N
Year of Birth	1917	1916	1915	1914	1913	1912	1911	1910	1909
	1926	1925	1924	1923	1922	1921	1920	1919	1918
	1935	1934	1933	1932	1931	1930	1929	1928	1927
	1944	1943	1942	1941	1940	1939	1938	1937	1936
	1953	1952	1951	1950	1949	1948	1947	1946	1945
	1962	1961	1960	1959	1958	1957	1956	1955	1954
	1971	1970	1969	1968	1967	1966	1965	1964	1963
	1980	1979	1978	1977	1976	1975	1974	1973	1972
	1989	1988	1987	1986	1985	1984	1983	1982	1981
	1998	1997	1996	1995	1994	1993	1992	1991	1990
	2007	2006	2005	2004	2003	2002	2001	2000	1999
	2016	2015	2014	2013	2012	2011	2010	2009	2008

Doing Business With Asians

*I*n trend-setting California, for the past several years the ten most frequent last names of home buyers include Lee, Wong, Kim and Nguyen. There has been a huge influx of immigrants from Asian countries in the last thirty years. People from these "traditional cultures" have different ways of doing business from the mostly European immigrants who preceded them.

These changes in demographics present the real estate industry with great opportunities as well as new challenges. Real estate professionals who understand these new business realities will be in a position to take advantage of the opportunities created by these new Asian buyers and sellers.

Unfortunately, denial is a fact of life. It is easy to stay in your comfort zone and explain away the changes by saying, "Immigrants like to do business with their own people" or, "Let's hire a few Chinese and a few Koreans and let them deal with their own people. We can never understand their culture." Avoiding the issue won't make it go away—but it will result in lost business and missed opportunites.

The expectations and behaviors of people who come from other cultures are influenced by a different set of rules. In order to do business successfully, you need to understand where the other side is coming from—the way they are used to conducting business, how they make decisions, and the best way to establish a relationship of trust and credibility. Your insights into their cultural values and belief systems will help both sides to be comfortable doing business and allow transactions to proceed smoothly without "cross-cultural noise."

Myths and Misconceptions

*B*efore we get into the specifics of doing business with Asians in the real estate business, let's clear up two basic miconceptions that serve as business-killing myths.

• *Myth #1: Foreign-born customers would rather do business with each other than with Americans.* I can think of several instances where this might be true: when there are language difficulties, or when they are obligated to do business with a relative or a friend. However, in the majority of cases they are looking for someone they can trust to give them the best service and terms.

And there are several compelling reasons why Asian immigrants often prefer to work with American-born professionals. Asians are very protective about their financial and personal information. Working with someone from their own cultural background risks leaking confidential knowledge back into their communities. They might also stay away from someone from the same community because they like to avoid incurring a heavy obligation or loss of face if things don't work out.

• *Myth #2: Asians don't want to learn the American way of doing business.* Invariably, someone during my seminars will ask me: "Since Asians are in this country, why don't they learn about our culture? Why do we have to learn about theirs?" These are valid questions.

The first answer is that their different way of doing things is not intentional. Culture to humans is like water to a fish. Cultural values are etched very deeply into our psyche; we are often unaware they are even there. We operate within a framework of learned survival skills that are out of our conscious awareness.

Second, doing business with the Asian community doesn't mean you have to abandon your ways of doing business and adopt theirs. But good customer service—especially in a highly competitive marketplace—means being sensitive to a client's needs. To be successful with Asian clients you need an awareness of cultural differences and what motivates their behavior and expectations. This awareness creates an atmosphere of comfort and confidence for both sides, instead of having you and them walking on egg shells, not knowing what to do next.

Four Key Cultural Differences

*F*our key cultural differences exist between mainstream American culture and traditional Asian cultures Gaining an understanding and empathy for these differences is crucial for businesspeople doing business in these communities.

• *Individualism vs. group orientation.* People from Asian cultures are more group oriented than most native-born Americans. A customer may arrive with several relatives or friends, and decisions are made within the group. In this country, responsibility for decisions lies with the individual. Although native-born Americans might consult with others on important decisions, such consultations are more limited in scope.

With foreign-born clients, you need to 1) be patient with the slower decision-making process, 2) be hospitable and gracious to family members and friends and include them when explaining the process and giving information, 3) let them feel at ease as they consult among themselves in their own language.

- *Informal vs. formal.* Americans value informality and equality over hierarchy and social class. Asian cultures are much more formal and hierarchical.

This means you need to be more formal when dealing with Asian customers. Address them by their last names and use titles such as Dr. Wong. They may call you by your first name if you have introduced yourself that way, but you should wait until they invite you to call *them* by their first names. This is especially important across gender lines.

- *Equality vs. Status.* People from traditional cultures like to do business with people of authority. The background and status of the individual who deals with them and the prestige of the organization mean a great deal. Businesspeople need to establish their authority and credentials and demonstrate competence in their field.

- *Direct vs. indirect.* "Don't beat around the bush" is a popular American axiom. In this culture quick and truthful information exchanges are valued. Traditional cultures value discretion and many things are left unsaid. Saving face and preventing humiliation on all sides may have a higher priority than being frank and upfront.

What people say is not always what they think. Instead of saying "no" they may say "It will be very difficult," or simply "maybe." Or they may tell you what they think you want to hear without any intention of going along.

Be careful not to be overly direct. For example, you don't want to look the customer straight in the face and say, "You don't make enough money to qualify for this loan amount!" or, "You can't afford this property, consider buying a less expensive one."

Instead, work out several examples of how the amount of initial investment plus monthly payments determine the price of the house that one can purchase. This indirectly communicates to them whether or not they are in the ball park.

Introductions

*H*andshaking is international business protocol, so you usually can't go wrong to extend your hand. However, if you are a man you may want to let female clients initiate the handshake. Some older people unaccustomed to doing business may not be used to shaking hands. Let them initiate the handshake.

Nonverbal Communication

*E*ach of us operates in a physical zone that is comfortable for us, but this zone differs widely among cultures. The United States is somewhere in the middle. Asians want a little more space. When I work with foreign-born customers, I remain stationary and let the other party choose how close they want to sit or stand.

•   *Physical contact.* Asians do not generally like physical contact and will generally be quite uncomfortable if you touch them during conversation.

•   *Dress.* Dress conservatively for business with Asian clients—and dress your best. Asian clients may not dress up when looking at properties, but don't let that fool you. You will gain their respect and make them more comfortable if you are professionally attired.

•   *Eye contact.* In Asian cultures, averting your eyes is a sign of respect. You should keep intense eye contact to a minimum when working with Asian clients.

Breaking the Ice

*T*he purpose of an ice-breaker is to bring down the walls that separate us and to establish a common bond. Unfortunately, as soon as we hear a foreign accent our curiosity takes over, and instead of establishing a common bond our first questions are likely to create walls. The following questions are a sure way to thicken the ice:

"Where are you from?"
"I can't tell Chinese from Koreans, which one are you?"
"How long have you been in this country?"
"When are you going back to your country?"
"Say something in Chinese."
"Oh, you are Japanese, I did business with a Korean couple. They came up with a large cash down payment."

Ice breakers should consist of light, pleasant, and nonemotional subjects. Weather, sporting events or other subjects which create a common bond or a shared experience are good ice breakers. The best ice-breaker is genuine warmth and hospitality.

Language and Accent Barriers

The problem with communication is the illusion that it has been accomplished.
—George Bernard Shaw

*T*he central problem with accents is the cadence and music of a language. When the music is unfamiliar we get distracted and can't hear the words. The trick is to listen very carefully—something most of us are not in the habit of doing—until you get used to the accent. Remember, accents are not always an indicator of language abilities; many people speak (and understand) English extremely well but still speak with an accent.

• *Avoid speaking loudly or emphasizing the words as if the other side is hard of hearing.* Be patient and allow them plenty of time to finish their sentence. When they are talking, don't impatiently rap on the table or fumble with your paperwork.

• *Repeat what your customer has just told you in your own words and summarize in a written memo to make sure everyone has understood.*

• *Using Interpreters.* When working with a client who has difficulty with English, it is preferable to get the help of someone who is knowledgeable about real estate terminology. If your customers bring in someone to act as a translator, you need to educate that person by defining the terminology needed for discussing all aspects of the deal.

• *Translations.* When translating documents and doing business with overseas clients, it is advisable to hire professionals to do the translating. Grabbing the closest person to you with the required native tongue is exposing your business to chance and miscommunication.

• *What sounds like rudeness probably isn't.* Sometimes the intonation of the customer's native language and lack of English ability can make them sound rude. But they are probably just self conscious about their language skills.

• *Telephone contacts.* Talking on the telephone is especially challenging when there's a foreign accent. Avoid getting into long conversations, trying to resolve complex issues or making sales on the phone. Make an appointment to see them in person instead.

The Value of Time

*P*eople from different cultures have different approaches to time and appointments. They may not be used to the highly scheduled punctuality of American life. If you have a 6 PM appointment, it might be a good idea to call that morning and confirm. Say how much you look forward to seeing them at six, and mention that you have another appointment at seven.

•   *Patience is an essential business skill.* People from traditional cultures may be less anxious to finish a business transaction quickly. They need time to consult with family members, negotiate and consider the deal from all angles.

How to Build Trust

*O*nce trust has been established, Asians tend to allow a real estate professional to guide and lead more than some native-born persons would. The most crucial element in doing business with foreign-born customers is establishing a relationship of confidence and trust.

Many people object, "I can't invest a lifetime in establishing a relationship. I need to make a living." But building a relationship of trust doesn't depend on time; it depends on your intent and your style. Here are some elements of establishing a relationship of trust across cultures:

•   *Express a sense of sincerity.* Sincerity means different things to Americans than it does to Asians. In this culture, if you are honest and upfront you are sincere. In traditional cultures, sincerity means having your client's best interests at heart. When they are sitting across the table from you, they need to feel you are working for them, not for some faceless company.

● *Avoid using pressure or being argumentative.*
Pressure undermines customers' trust in you. A better
strategy is to give the information that focuses their attention
on the deal and helps them make a decision.

● *Keep your word as though it's a written contract.*
Don't "shoot from the hip." If you don't have the information
at hand, tell them you'll get back to them later. Be consistent
about what you say and promise to do.

● *Establish rapport.* Don't rush to do business the
instant you meet a prospect. First, establish a rapport. Avoid
cross-examining an Asian client. Don't rush with the facts.

How to Build Credibility

*T*o establish trust you need to project credibility. A good word about you from a trusted friend or a relative establishes instant credibility. Hence the importance of networking and referrals.

• *Present your credentials in writing.* Before attempting to do business, communicate your expertise and your background. This information should be in a resume or a personal brochure. Talking about yourself is viewed as bragging or boasting in many traditional cultures.

• *Establish rank and status.* Asians like to do business with people of authority. The trappings of rank and status go a long way toward establishing credibility with clients from these cultures. Titles such as "vice president" or "manager" assure them you have the authority and professional skills needed to help them.

Hospitality

*I*n Asian cultures, hospitality is very important. When clients come into your office, it is very important to offer them tea, coffee or some other refreshment. People from Asia may tell you to please not bother—but it's your job to insist a couple of times.

Be Positive

*T*he Asian market is large and can be quite lucrative. You'll find that customers who are happy with your service will give you more referrals than you might see from Anglo clients.

Approach this market with a positive attitude. Human beings are much more similar than they are different. When you understand and value someone's cultural differences, then you can get past them to concentrate on the similarities. If you show good faith, they will overlook small mistakes you might make.

Negotiation and Bargaining

*I*n this country, we don't tend to negotiate except in buying cars and homes. People who come from Asian cultures may have negotiated all their lives. They tend to like negotiating. They usually expect to negotiate. They may come in with very low offers. If you're the selling agent, don't get exasperated. They just want to make sure that they're getting the best deal possible. If you're the listing agent, educate your sellers. Encourage them to counter.

I recently saw a salesperson at a seminar who had previously taken one of my courses. He wanted to tell me a success story. He said that he's a heavy lister and in the past when he's gotten very low offers from Asians on property, he hadn't always encouraged his insulted sellers to counter.

After hearing my seminar, he received a very low offer and after calming his sellers down, encouraged them to counter, coming down very little. The buyers came up a lot, and the property closed. The associate said it was a transaction that he would have thrown away in the past.

Using This Knowledge

*O*ur discussions of cultural differences have given you valuable insights for more successful business transactions. Having had this education, you are now able to graduate to the next level—where you focus on the similarities instead on the differences.

All of us respond to our commonalties much more than to our differences. Learning about differences enables you to build a bridge to the common ground where business can be done.

You can reap the benefits of doing business with an increasingly affluent Asian-American population by celebrating our commonalities and building bridges to bring us together with a shared stake in a common society. Successful business relationships start a positive cycle of good feelings that benefit all of us, both professionally and personally.

Conclusion

This book has given you an outline of feng shui concepts such as yin and yang, ch'i, balance and harmony. Of course, there's a lot more to learn. But it isn't necessary that you understand all the nuances and mysteries of feng shui. Your customers probably don't either. That's why there are feng shui masters.

What this book provides is a basic set of reference points so that you can feel comfortable talking with Asian customers about the good points and problems of a property from a feng shui perspective.

Remember that many feng shui rules resulted from common-sense solutions to problems of everyday living. Most people in the northern hemisphere prefer a south-facing home. Nobody wants to walk in the front door and come face to face with a toilet bowl. Properly proportioned windows and doors make a house feel balanced and welcoming. Hills and water views are desired by most people.

In the end, a home, office or restaurant in which you feel comfortable and which shows a sense of proportion and good taste probably has good feng shui. The rules of feng shui are, in the final analysis, a way of talking about these intuitive feelings we have about the places we live and work.

Remember also that not all Asians believe in feng shui— at least not explicitly. But many have been influenced by feng shui traditions and folklore. Even if the buyer or seller does not believe in feng shui, there are often relatives or others involved in the deal who do.

Some people will be forthcoming and profess their beliefs and preferences. Others will keep their preferences to themselves. The best rule when dealing with Asian clients is to approach the matter in an indirect way. Postpone direct questions about feng shui until you know them better or until they bring up the subject themselves.

It's a good idea, however, to demonstrate that you are conscious of feng shui principles by asking the right questions about location, orientation, design and other preferences. As you reveal your feng shui awareness and knowledge, your clients will often open up about their own beliefs and preferences. But even if they don't, they will respect your knowledge of the subject.

A Final Word of Caution

Not all Asians believe in feng shui. To assume they do might offend them. You need to approach this subject with sensitivity and let them tell you their preferences.

About the Author

Sheida Hodge is president of Professional Training Worldwide, which provides training and consulting services in three main areas: 1) helping business executives to become more effective in the global marketplace by providing country-specific training in sales, customer service, team-building, and negotiations, 2) helping businesses improve their customer service and increase their sales in the growing ethnic and immigrant markets in the United States, 3) providing a simulation-based negotiating skills program that applies to both domestic and international markets.

Ms. Hodge has extensive experience in doing business internationally. She was responsible for international business development and U.S. distribution programs for industrial products with General Electric Company, with responsibilities in Asia, South America, Europe, and the Middle East. She also built a successful import business which she later sold to an overseas manufacturer.

Ms. Hodge has an MBA degree and a BS in mathematics. She developed courses in Global Business Skills for the Extension Program for Executive Development at UCLA and a course in Effective International Negotiating for the

University of California, Irvine. She has trained executives from Boeing, Allergan, Bell Helicopter Textron, Applied Materials, Cubic Corporation, American Skandia, Inc. and Northrop Grumman just to name a few.

An internationally recognized speaker, Ms. Hodge frequently addresses major real estate conventions across the U.S. and Canada. She has published numerous articles about doing business across cultures. She has also produced a best-selling video entitled "Secrets of Successful Cross-Cultural Marketing." Readers interested in contacting Ms. Hodge about speaking or conducting seminars can reach her at:

Tel: (949) 250-0856

Fax: (949) 250-0711

E-mail: Sheida_Hodge@compuserve.com

Additional Feng Shui Readings

Feng-Shui: The Chinese Art of Placement.
   Sarah Rossbach, Arkansas Press, 1983.

The Living Earth Manual of Feng-Shui.
   Stephen Skinner, Arkana Press, 1982.

Feng Shui: A Layman's Guide to Chinese Geomancy.
   Evelyn Lip, Heian International, Inc.

Feng Shui for the Home.
   Evelyn Lip, Heian International, Inc., 1990.

Feng Shui for Business.
   Evelyn Lip, Heian International, Inc., 1990.

The Feng Shui Handbook.
   Derek Walters, Aquarian Press, 1991.

The Western Guide to Feng Shui.
   Terah Kathryn Collins, Hay House, Inc., 1996.

The Complete Illustrated Guide to Feng Shui.
   Lillian Too, Barnes & Noble, Inc., 1996.

The Principles of Feng Shui.
   The American Feng Shui Institute.